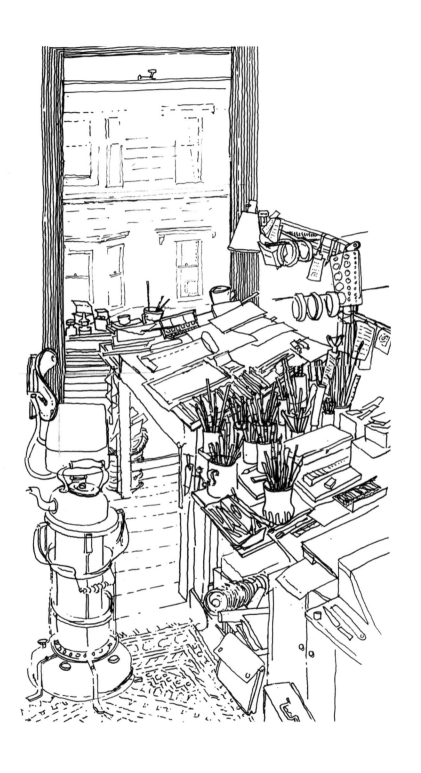

The studio at Joan's Cranworth Street flat where she lived from 1950 until 1988. Pen and Ink

JOAN RIX TEBBUTT

ARTIST AND SCRIBE
1910 – 2005

Edited by
SUE HAMILTON

Foreword by
PAUL HEPPLESTON

ISBN 0-9553554-0-0
ISBN 978-0-9553554-0-0

Front Cover: *Four Gospels*. Gold Tooling on Vellum.

First published in 2006
by the Executors of the Estate of Joan Rix Tebbutt,
3 Charles Court, Limekilns, Fife, KY11 3LG

Printed in Great Britain by Inglis Allen,
Kirkcaldy, Fife, Scotland.

Editor's Preface

It has been my privilege to compile this edition of Joan's work.

Apart from the vellum bindings, very little of the work illustrated here has been published before. This compilation largely reflects Joan's approach to continuous innovation through every phase of her artistic life. It does not attempt to catalogue a sequential development but, rather, reflects the intensely personal and creative way in which she related to her subjects.

The intention is that this book, sitting on many bookshelves, will serve as a dispersed memorial to Joan. It is by no means an exhaustive record of her work.

Much of the text is in the voices of others (whom I have acknowledged). I hope I have done them justice in the use I have made of their contributions. I would particularly like to mention the perspectives provided by James Brockman, Alan Farant and Faith Shannon on Joan's collaboration with Sandy Cockerell. I would also like to thank Sue Hufton of The Society of Scribes and Illuminators and Gerald Fleuss of the Edward Johnson Foundation for encouraging me to embark upon this tribute to Joan. The production of this book has been made so much easier through the help, encouragement and advice given freely by Lucina Prestige, Eddie Ross of Inglis Allen and my husband, Malcolm.

The text is printed throughout in Optima. In a pencilled note among her papers, Joan writes:

'OPTIMA – seized on by Sandy and me as soon as invented in 1958'. On the same page she quotes from Stanley Morison (typographer 1889 – 1967):

'For a font to be successful, it has to be so good that only very few recognise its novelty'.

Sue Hamilton

Foreword

Joan was born in Glasgow in 1910, the daughter of Gwen Rix and Arthur Tebbutt. It is important to understand Gwen, for only then can one understand Joan, as she was inspired by her mother from start to finish. Gwen was Joan's role model and her point of reference. It is from her that Joan received so much that directed her own life.

Gwen was, without doubt, a woman far ahead of her time, a person of great wisdom and energy and enlightened thinking. As a Christian Socialist, she was at the forefront of the new way of thought in the early 20th century, a move towards justice for all and a richness of experience for her children. Gwen's firm ideas extended to the education of her children, who were regularly moved from school to school to ensure that they received educational experiences in accord with Gwen's philosophy. Joan always expressed a certain pride in having been expelled from Hillhead High School for her mother's refusal to allow her to wear uniform. Gwen's approach to their schooling brought either derision (*'Look what she's doing to her children!'*) or astonished admiration (*'Look what she's doing for her children!'*).

Gwen's brother Edwin, a non-conformist minister, wrote of Gwen:

'A deeply religious woman, she lived with her husband and family on the edge of one of the gloomiest parts of Glasgow. From their earliest childhood, she turned her children's faces from the crowded streets to the beauty of the Scottish mountains and the surrounding sea. At Portavadie she made them master a simple, hard life and her children shall bless her every time they sail a boat or climb a mountain. She loved flowers, in garden and in vase, and her mind would always search for beauty and for truth. Above all, her belief in Christ remained deep and usually silent - often assailed but always unshaken'.

Joan loved the beauty and truth of poetry. She wrote one
particularly moving piece to her father in 1947, a year after
Gwen's early death

OCTOBER AGAIN

October again – and it is now a year
since you walked out and shut the door,
leaving us entangled in your words. Your mind
lives on in the garden and your eyes look down,
smiling, from the copper pot you loved;
and we still drink from your yellow cup.
It is a year now since they found your tired body
lying on the ground;
and yet we know by some recurring word,
or look caught unawares, that you still drive
our thoughts like the smart cobs of your youth,
when you and the world were alive.

   Like Gwen, Joan's spirituality was real, deep, unspoken but
living. Joan hardly ever <u>spoke</u> of God, but she wrote of God
in her artwork again and again, quoting poets and religious
thinkers through <u>their</u> words on <u>her</u> vellum. Joan knew from
experience the huge difference between religiosity and faith.
She knew too the difference between falsehood and genuine-
ness; that's why she needed Portavadie. Glasgow life required
an antidote of peace and tranquillity, a retreat from a constant
and hectic life with people. At the caravan she found escape,
solace and, above all, a re-connecting with Gwen's approach to
living with nature, on nature's terms. That way was possible at
Portavadie. Family members try to continue that way at Stillaig,
not to maintain a morbid memorial to Joan, but because that
way of life is worth living for itself in a world where truth and
values seem to have deteriorated so very much.

Paul Heppleston

Joan Rix Tebbutt 1910 – 2005

Joan was a student at Glasgow School of Art, which was to become *'the heart of my life'*. She studied calligraphy under Ailsa Craig and was awarded a Diploma in Lettering and Book Design in 1933.

After leaving Glasgow School of Art, Joan taught in various schools in Glasgow including 'Hutchies'. She is remembered there by Anne McGavin:

'I can see myself at the top of the stairs waiting outside the Art Room. I felt awkward and tall among my peers. As Joan arrived to take the class, her face lit up as she beamed at me and said "Oh, what a nice tall person you are!" She had a gift of giving approval when it was most needed.'

During the Second World War, Joan went to teach in Keswick where she developed her love of the Lake District and its mountains, which she climbed with members of the Fell and Rock Climbing Club. Her success as a teacher is evident in the number of her former pupils who remained friends. She not only inspired pupils and students into adventure and exploration of their artistic side, but through her passion for mountains and the sea, introduced many of them to the hills, to cooking on a campfire, and to the spiritual fulfilment of the outdoors.

Of her climbing in Scotland, Douglas Scott writes:

'In these early years, Joan was athletic and a very enthusiastic climber. When she wasn't sketching or painting, she would be climbing on the Campsies or cycling to Arrochar to climb the The Cobbler. Later, the most exciting prospect for Joan was of a day on one of the old classic climbs, The Tower Ridge on Ben Nevis or the Aonach Eagach or, in winter, a good snow route like Ben Lui Gully. These, she climbed with some of the leading men in the Scottish Mountaineering Club. She did some pretty spectacular climbing with women too – including the Cuillin Ridge on Skye in 1938'.

Joan in her element at Portavadie - aged four.

In the Brown Tent at Portavadie. Pen and ink.

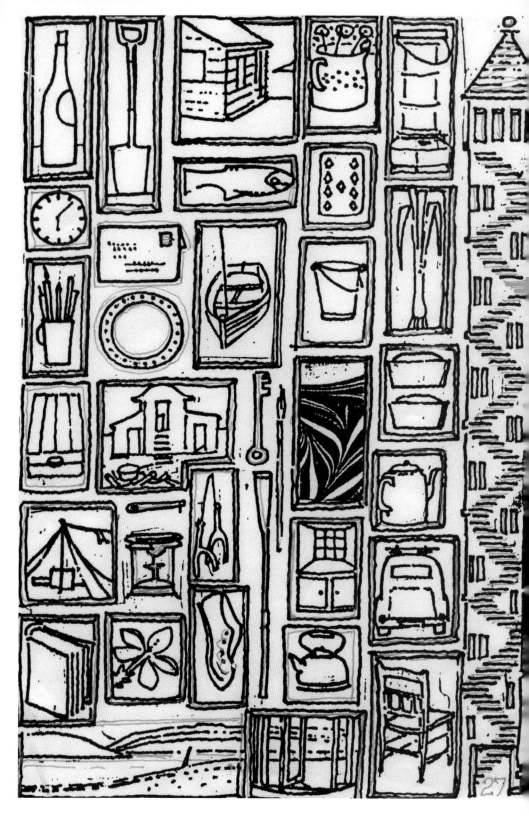

27

Douglas Scott continues,

'When she returned to Scotland to live, she took to skiing with great enthusiasm and enjoyed the exhilaration of descent, often after walking up on 'skins'. A bad fall on Meall a Bhuiridh led to the end of this, her best-loved outdoor activity. (Typically, she told no one of her injuries and carried down her own skis)'.

In 1947 she took up a teaching post at St Bride's School in Helensburgh where she remained for the next 16 years. The artist, Rosalind Bliss recalls:

'When I was setting out for St Brides in 1950, my father (D P Bliss, director of Glasgow School of Art 1946 – 1964) told me that I was going to have "the best art teacher in Scotland"! So any expectations were great and were not disappointed. Joan was brim full of life and energy, and ideas for ways and means of doing things'.

Janet Barnes was similarly inspired.

'She had a remarkable gift for making the visual world intelligible and exciting to children. Her art room was always full of amazing visual images, posters, reproductions, an astounding range of coloured textiles, plants, food, and treasures of all kinds. Design was central to her art curriculum: all her pupils were taught the elements of printmaking, bookbinding, linocutting and lettering. Her recognition of her pupils' work was summed up in her repeated remark to students "I have taught you nothing". She could see an innate gift for what it was - and thus acknowledged that the teacher often became the pupil'.

Opposite: *Iconography*. Pen and inks.

Joan's perspectives on Art

Notes that Joan made for a lecture to sixth year girls and their parents before they left St Brides provide some interesting insights into Joan's philosophy and teaching:

On being a designer

A painter can afford to make mistakes – he is answerable only to himself. A designer can't. He has to do right by other people.

On the word 'Art'

'Art' is a useful wee word where timetables are concerned – it takes so little room. But it always rather shakes me to see it casually scribbled as 'Art 2.30 - 3.30'. It stands for something so immense, so far reaching, so all-embracing, so SUBTLE - like all those other huge awesome realities that are named in our language with such tiny words: life, love, death, sun, moon, sky, hills, earth, sleep, tree, rock, wood, rain.

On boring teachers

And if I get a bit irritatingly teacherish, you can always do what the children do when the seats get hard, ask some (ir)relevant question, ask for leave, or to go to music, or take a neighbour out feeling faint.

On the merits of charcoal

An inch or two of charcoal and an entire Glasgow Herald will keep a child happy on the floor for hours. But be sure to pin it down well at the corners (the Glasgow Herald, I mean). You can get unprinted newspaper very cheaply and a wad of this pinned to a board should keep you happy for hours.

On composing

When a composer writes a piece of music, he is dealing with TIME – dividing it up into silences and sounds at certain intervals. The silences and sounds use up just that 20 minutes. In composing a picture, you are dividing a rectangular area into space and mass; and the relation between the four bounding lines and the shapes within is extremely important. But so little of this is recognised (or taught), that beginners inevitably think of putting things into a space, like putting biscuits on a plate. They are thinking far more of the subject, in fact, than the pattern which must be the basis of every picture.

On modern inventions

The debasement of writing occurred when the first flexible pen was introduced, and lately the ballpoint – both in the cause of speed.

But now, that there are writing machines for those that need speed, we can get back to clear traditional forms and make a new start. In the same way, the camera has freed artists from the need to make their pictures photographically realistic.

On Art in everyone's life

You may feel that no further demands may ever be made on you to draw or paint. But, there is no question of giving up Art - any more than giving up Life. Not a day in your life will pass without your having to come to some decision about proportion, colour, spatial relationships, texture. Something of your taste comes into these things every time you lay plates on the table and, of course, when you arrange the flowers, place the vases, dust the mantelpiece and put the ornaments back.

On the distinction between 'Good' and 'Beautiful'

There is always a right and a wrong relationship, a good and a bad way of placing things. You notice how much more often this word 'good' is used than the word 'beautiful'. 'Beauty' is difficult of definition and has been very much overused according to fashion and personal taste. So a carpenter, looking at a chair, a boat builder at the sheer line of a deck, a dressmaker at the set of a sleeve, a producer appraising a play will say: 'That is good' (or 'That is bad'), not 'That is beautiful' (or 'That is ugly'); so also will a painter in front of a picture, meaning that the paint, or whatever the material is, has been handled with skill and suitability, with special respect for the material itself and with love for its intrinsic worth, rather than concealing bad work with over-ornament or making one thing pretend it's another. One could almost define Art as all hand-work done with love, interest and care for quality.

Opposite: Cover design for Hill Farming Research Organisation Report. Lino cut. 1964.

HILL FARMING
research organisation

THIRD REPORT

Glasgow School of Art

In 1964, after many years teaching in schools, Joan accepted an invitation from Harry Barnes, the recently appointed principal, to teach at Glasgow School of Art. Here she became a member of a teaching team of artists and designers responsible for this first important rung on the ladder for professional artists. Harry Barnes wrote, (in his introduction to *Thirty Recent Bindings* in 1981)

'The experience of the next ten years had, I believe a great significance on her own development as a designer. As a young woman she was both inspired and influenced by Eric Gill, his use of lettering and illustration in the overall creation of an inscription or a book. Although later she lost sympathy with the content of much of Gill's work, this initial admiration remained and became something personal to Joan. Like almost every other scribe of her generation, she was influenced by the work of Edward Johnson, but she never became obsessed with the niceties of form to the exclusion of the need to communicate the whole message effectively; and never to the exclusion of a certain light-hearted wit and fantasy when this was appropriate.

She was a mature artist by the time she came to work at the School of Art and up to that time one might have said that her skill as a draughtsman or decorator, apart from her skill as a calligrapher and scribe, had remained essentially figurative and naturalistic. Because she is a natural teacher and because she established such a splendid rapport with many of the brighter students who passed through her hands, I think in a subtle but quite unselfconscious way, Joan absorbed a new confidence, almost a new liberation of her own abilities as a designer, but in sympathy and accord with this generation rather than her own'.

Sheep on the isthmus. Watercolour.

Cover design for the Hill Farming Research Organisation.
Self-adhesive textured film and pen and ink.

Cir Mhor. Self-adhesive textured film.

My shadow cast across the snow and onto the hill beyond. Watercolour.

18

Arriving at Portavadie. Pastel.

Wild flowers. Pen and ink.

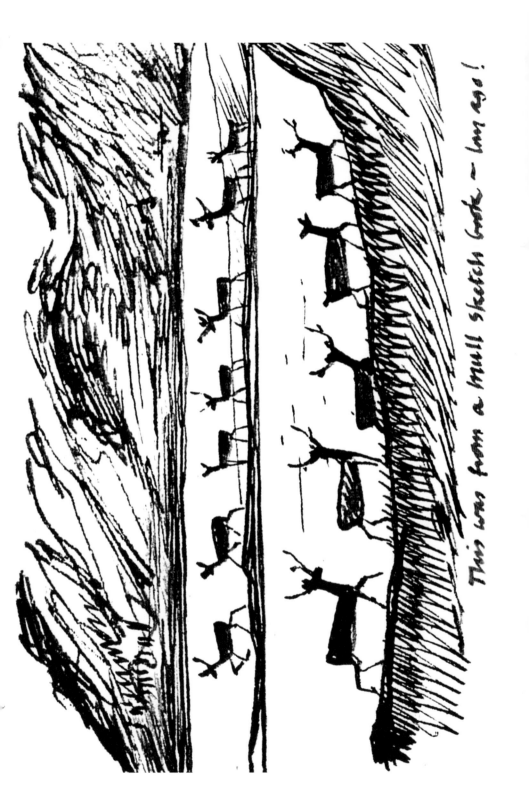

This was from a small sketch book — long ago!

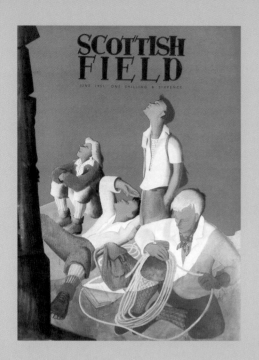

Scottish Field cover designs. Watercolour.

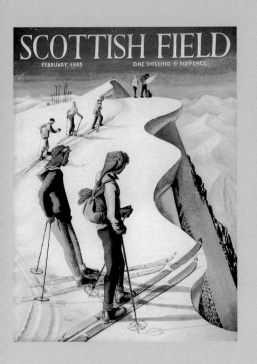

Scottish Field cover designs. Watercolour.

Working with Sandy Cockerell

Joan met Sandy (Sidney Morris Cockerell) in the 1940s and became a significant member of his bookbinding community, first at Letchworth and then at Riversdale, near Cambridge. As well as producing traditional bindings of very high quality, Sandy repaired ancient and rare books and produced handmade marbled papers. In her tribute to Sandy, printed in *The Scribe* of Summer 1988, Joan described - with typical modesty - her own input into the work.

'These vellum books were the ones that concerned me. Long ago Sandy had noticed ink lettering, and some decoration, on a papyrus account book of about 700 AD and suggested we try this idea out together. I was a fairly raw sort of scribe and this was the beginning of a lot of learning for me - just to be doing things in such a workshop was an education'. This typifies Joan's generosity, never taking the limelight, no matter how much it was deserved. Joan learnt from Sandy the constraints on book design imposed by traditional tools and the techniques of gilding and lettering. Sandy gradually learnt from Joan that they could, together, acquire freedom from these constraints. She created designs that needed new tools and new techniques. Sandy responded with typical ingenuity, by inventing them.

Alan Farrant worked at the Riversdale bindery. He remembers that Joan would come to Cambridge (often driving down in her open-top Morris Minor from Glasgow) to spend several weeks working with Sandy. To save time, much preliminary work had already been done before she arrived. Watercolour sketches, samples pieces from the skins and ideas for lettering designs had been posted back and forth between Cambridge and Glasgow.

'We all looked forward to Joan's arrival, and admired her apparent independence, her immense skill at her craft, and the very warmth of her personality.

She engaged us in a manner which we, as a relatively young group of people, would perhaps not experience elsewhere, particularly with others of a slightly older generation. Joan's opinions and ideas proved to be a vital ingredient in the life of the workshop, even though for most of the year she was in Scotland.'

James Brockman, the bookbinder, who also worked with Sandy, describes the challenges of working with vellum. 'Vellum is a mechanical material - which can be much more amenable than leather. But you do need to have a relationship with it. It's very brittle. Other people wet it, but then you can get warping of the boards. Sandy applied it dry like a thin sheet of metal or veneer. He had a standing order with Cowleys, the suppliers of skins, to keep the most interestingly marked skins for him. Joan was very influential in the choice of a particular skin and her designs would be developed to complement the markings on the skin. Getting the brushed Indian ink to stick to the vellum was another problem – you could sand it with garnet sandpaper, but the extent to which the ink adhered could also be a function of the age of the goat!'

Sandy invented gadgets that made it possible to tool vellum – a process that, hitherto, had rarely been attempted because the material is so hard. He understood how to achieve the right amount of plastic flow in the skin when using hot tools. He made shaped brass tools to apply the simple gold elements of Joan's designs. The heated tools were applied to the vellum with a ram. ('The ram is made from an aircraft flap which is attached to the ceiling by a ball and socket joint ....') Lettering on the spines required very special measures. Sandy created a three-legged gadget that held a book virtually in Joan's lap so that she could apply her exquisite ink-brushed lettering onto the spines of the books.'

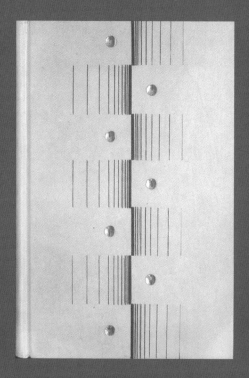

Iron Honey Gold. 1972.
Ruled black ink lines and tooled gold dots on vellum binding.

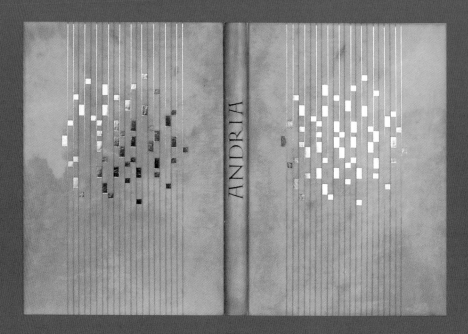

Andria. 1976. Tooled gold lines and rectangles on vellum binding.

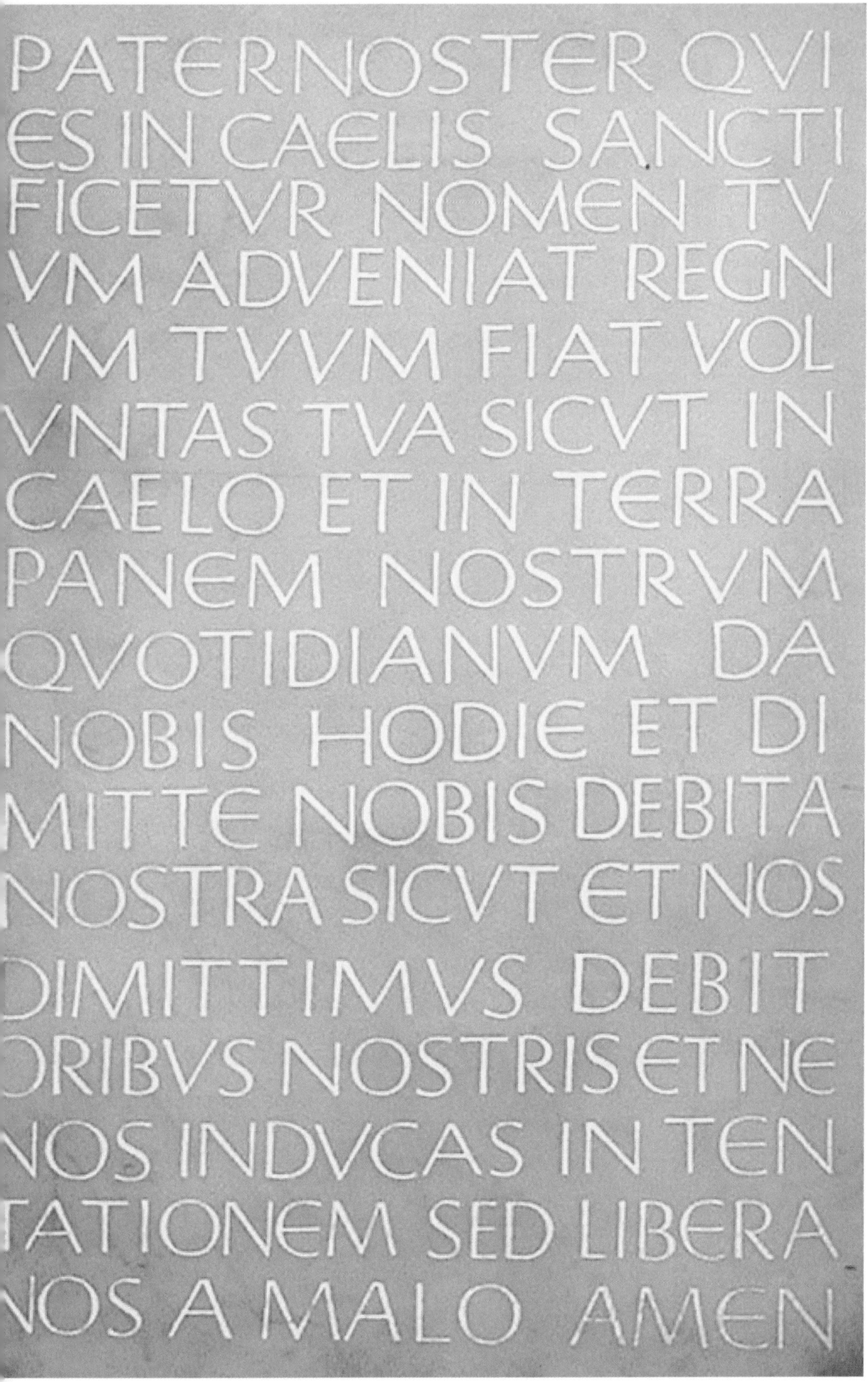

PATERNOSTER QVI
ES IN CAELIS SANCTI
FICETVR NOMEN TV
VM ADVENIAT REGN
VM TVVM FIAT VOL
VNTAS TVA SICVT IN
CAELO ET IN TERRA
PANEM NOSTRVM
QVOTIDIANVM DA
NOBIS HODIE ET DI
MITTE NOBIS DEBITA
NOSTRA SICVT ET NOS
DIMITTIMVS DEBIT
ORIBVS NOSTRIS ET NE
NOS INDVCAS IN TEN
TATIONEM SED LIBERA
NOS A MALO AMEN

The extraordinary collaboration between Joan, the designer, and Sandy, the craftsman, culminated in the production of a collection of exquisite vellum bindings for a series of rare books, commissioned by Colin Hamilton and Kulgin Duval.

Faith Shannon, another contemporary bookbinder, provides vivid images of this very productive partnership between Joan and Sandy.

'It is often the case that a designer of a binding will have their design interpreted by the finisher. With Joan and Sandy's bindings, the design and finish processes were quite inseparable. The liaison was very particular and very fruitful. They respected each other, and each had a close understanding of how the other person worked. There was cohesion and oneness. Sandy understood supremely how he could facilitate Joan's ideas. What happened here could only have occurred between these two people. He had the skills and the craftsmanship and the understanding to make Joan's ideas work. There was tremendous refinement. It just was supremely right. Neither Sandy nor Joan could have developed in any of the ways they did without the other. Joan was strong but winsome – and an intellectual.'

On hearing the news of Sandy's death in 1987 Joan said *'The landscape has changed now, where once was a great oak now only an empty sky'*. The same can now be said of Joan.

A collection of Cockerell – Tebbutt bindings was first exhibited as *Thirty Recent Bindings* at the Fitzwilliam Museum in Cambridge in 1981. A further collection of the bindings was exhibited at the Gallery of Modern Art in Glasgow in 1998 in *Joan Rix Tebbutt – Artist and Calligrapher*. Most recently they were again exhibited in *Books Which We Think You Might Enjoy Binding* at The Dean Gallery in Edinburgh in September 2004.

Previous Page. *Paternoster*. Binding for *Sermo Domini in Monte*. *1980*.

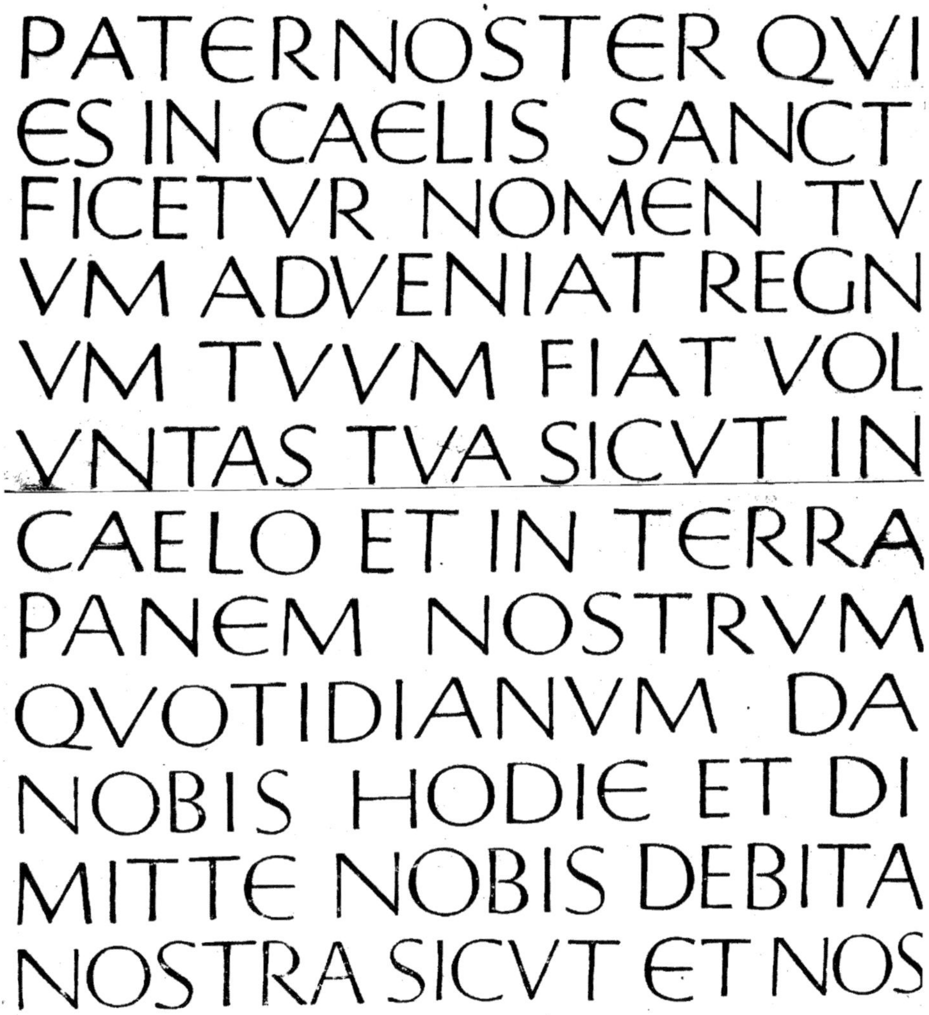

PATERNOSTER QVI
ES IN CAELIS SANCT
FICETVR NOMEN TV
VM ADVENIAT REGN
VM TVVM FIAT VOL
VNTAS TVA SICVT IN
CAELO ET IN TERRA
PANEM NOSTRVM
QVOTIDIANVM DA
NOBIS HODIE ET DI
MITTE NOBIS DEBITA
NOSTRA SICVT ET NOS

Draft for *Paternoster*, showing how the lettering in two of the three
separate blocks had to be seamlessly aligned.

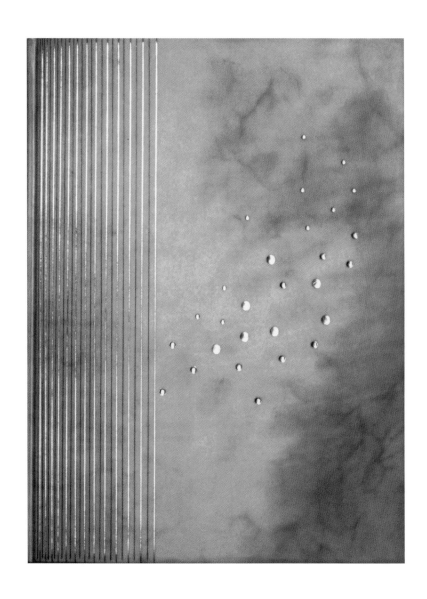

Eclogues. 1979. The first binding commissioned
by Colin Hamilton and Kulgin Duval.
Gold and black lines and gold circles on vellum.

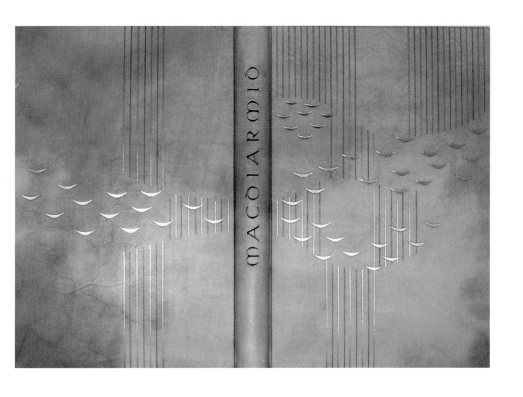

MacDiarmid. 1985. Gold tooling and black ink on vellum.

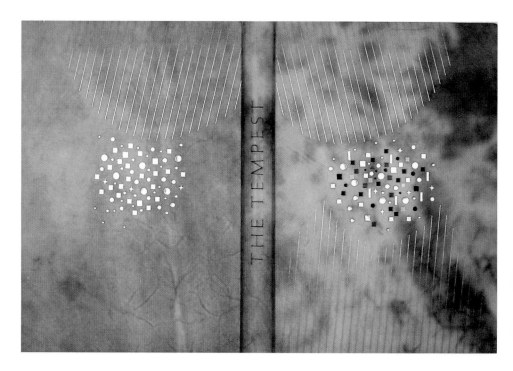

The Tempest. 1985. Gold and coloured tooling on heavily figured vellum.

Joan Tebbutt with Sandy and Elizabeth Cockerell
in the bindery at Riversdale. 1981.

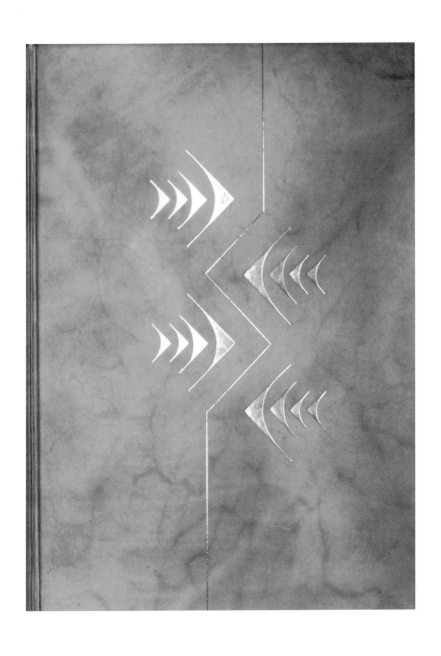

Four Gospels. 1979. Gold tooling on vellum.

'Joan's fine lettering on the spines is among the most beautiful in books of any period'. Indian ink on vellum.

34

WHITEMANED SEAHORSES CHAMPING BRIGHTWINDBRIDLED THE STEEDS OF MANANAAN

Words from James Joyce's *Ulysses*. Gold leaf on vellum panel.

Coloured and gold rectangles. Vellum panel.

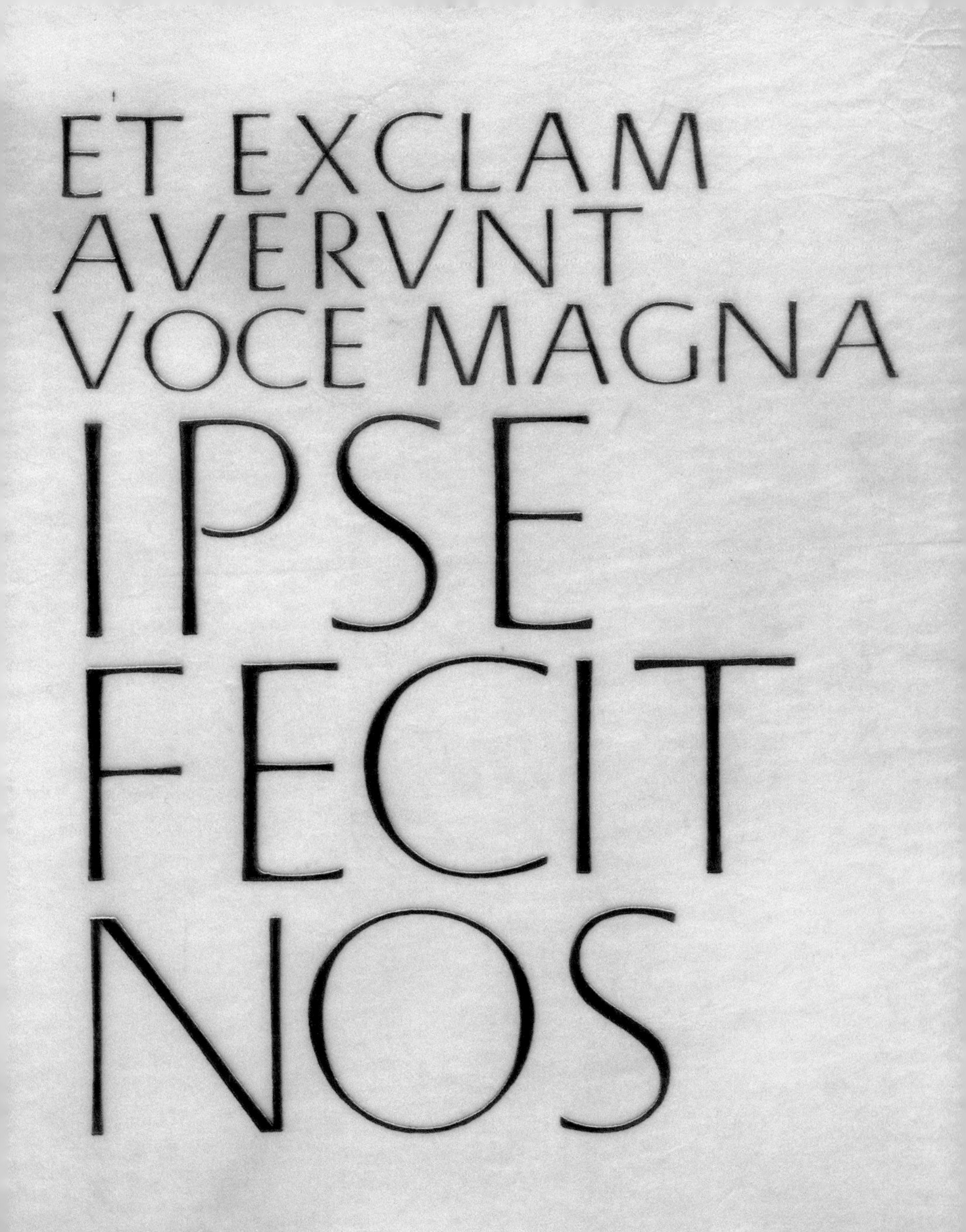

ET EXCLAM
AVERVNT
VOCE MAGNA
IPSE
FECIT
NOS

From *The Confessions of St Augustine*. Gold leaf on vellum panel.

Etonnante Peinture. Black and red ink on paper.
Louis Gillet 1927, observations on Monet's *Water Lilies*.

WHAT'S IN AN EGG?

A song is there, in chemical notation
   Invisibly packed into the genes.
Also detailed instructions for nest building
   A menu or two and a map of stars—
All in one cell that multiplies into many,
   All put at the disposal
Of the little feathered passenger:
   So, once hatched, and fledged,
He will have more than a wishbone—
   To launch his life.

GUY MURCHIE

What's in an Egg? Black and red ink on paper.

Greeting card for Sandy and Elizabeth. Ink and watercolour.

40

Sandy's door. Ink and collage.

REMEMBERING
SANDY

who understood books
and Books ———— writing &
Writing ———— Scribes and
binders and paper and
vellum and gold
Wings and fur & water
& fire and roofs
and wind and stone
and keels and sails
& ladders & tools ———
and Tools ——— & linen &
rope ——— and walls
and locks & skins
& clocks ——— & squares
and roots and trees
& rain and pumps and
light ——— & flight &
beginnings and
ends ——— & fun

Part of a review of Stravinsky's *Right of Spring* from the
Boston Herald 6 February 1924. Black and red ink on paper.

Cornice. Felt pen.

A development, in colour, of the design used on the
cover of *Hills of Lakeland* by Heaton Cooper.
Felt pen and watercolour.

Primrose. Flower Series 1979.
Stamp, pen and ink.

Glenfinnan. National
Trust Series 1981. Stamp,
watercolour, pen and ink.

Primrose. Flower Series.
1979. Stamp and collage.

Snowdrop. Flower Series.
1979. Stamp, pen and ink.

Works incorporating Royal Mail postage stamps

Grass of Parnassus. Watercolour.

Mountain skyline. Watercolour across two pages in a sketchbook.

Anemone de Caen. Pen and ink,
watercolour.

Japanese anemones. Watercolour.

Etoile d'Hollande. Collage of coloured tissue paper, paper, and white paint.

Yellow jasmine. Pen and ink and watercolour.

Window with yellow jasmine at Top House. Watercolour, tissue paper and instructions to place a candle behind it.

Door at Top House. Watercolour, tissue paper and instructions to place a candle behind it.

Top House. Lino cut.

Top House. Pencil on back of envelope.

Design for Parameswaran's® Pepper label and bag.
Front and reverse.

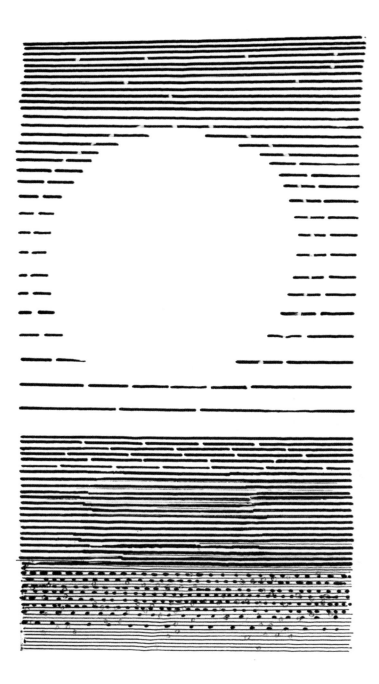

*Moon, stars, and twinkling reflections
on the sea and shingle.* Pen and ink.

Epilogue

As is amply illustrated in these pages, Joan's artistic skills were manifold and infinitely creative. She moved between pen and ink, watercolour, lino cut, pastel, gold leaf, collage with textured adhesive film, and collage with coloured tissue paper. Her adventures in lettering were similarly experimental and inventive. She went on absorbing new ideas throughout her life until with the devastating onset of blindness, Joan regretted that she could no longer *see what is most important to me - line with line, shape, form, pattern'*.

Joan's later years were devoted to family, to friends and to her allotment. She cooked and talked and gardened well into her nineties. The beautiful books, the pieces of exquisite calligraphy, the many sketches and paintings provide a lasting legacy of this most remarkable woman. Joan shared her life with scores of different individuals. The mention of her name will, forever, elicit treasured memories from each person whose life she touched. They will remember Joan with warm affection, not only because of her skills and gifts so amply illustrated here, but because she brought light, beauty and fun into their lives.

Words spoken at Joan's funeral by her niece, Ruth

Sight   What Joan could see and how things looked
mattered so much to her. The pattern of things.
High hills, reflected in headlands and then in islands.
Mountains and the wide skies at their tops.
Shorelines.
Sunset over Tarbert. Sunrise from Cleveden Drive.
Shine of mica schist.
Phosphorescence dripping from the oars at night.
The boat at her mooring with fine lines of mast, stem and
rake. Joan's drawings of herself going to sea. Setting sail,
independent, in control – and vulnerable.
Her writing. Lettering on bindings and vellum.
The Christmas Cards.
Her letters. Oh, what letters they were. And special
letters to her sister Nan.
The books she shared. The cuttings she kept.

Hearing   The sound of Joan's laughter. Phone calls,
including their silences. More laughter.
Voices of Colin, Edward, Nan.
Voices from Joan's own past, Gwen and Bob, Edwin,
Thella, who were saints for her.
We echo to her lifesounds.
The sea. The wind. Rain on a tent or on still sea.
The scrunch of footsteps on the shingle.
A primus roaring, a fire crackling and the whistling kettle.
Oystercatchers. Gulls on Yellow Isle. Fishing boats out of
Tarbert at night.
Bach and Mozart.
And the sound that isn't silence - 'the rushing stillness'.

Smell   The scent of lavender. Roger & Gallet cologne.
Carnation soap. Sweet peas, stocks and roses at the plot.
Good coffee.
Sandy's workshop – paper, ink, vellum. Tobacco. Sharpened
pencils. Paint.
Portavadie memories – the smell of the dark dairy, warm
cows, milk cooling against the smell of hot dry summer days.
Varnished wood of the dinghy.
The sea, the shore, seaweed. Sphagnum and leaf mould
in walks through the woods. Heather, crushed bracken.
Woodsmoke.
Above and around all, Bog Myrtle.

Taste   Early memories of tea made in a kettle over a
camp fire (before teabags),
Tarbert kippers, chanterelles, Kendal Mint Cake on a hill.
Later, Green and Black chocolate, bramble jelly, redcurrants
frosted with sugar, raspberries, the cream jug,
Vignotte. Joan's soup, her macaroons, her bread,
and her lemonade.
At Wardside, new potatoes with mint cooked on a primus
outside,
smoked salmon sandwich, and, at the very end, ice cream...

Touch   Bare feet on shingle or short turf, on the wooden
floor of the caravan, on the stones at the Hut.
Sandshoes on the stone stairs at Cranworth Street. Boots
firmly holding to rock, hand holds.
Roughness of rope. Smoothed wood from the shore.
Sticks placed by careful hand for a kettle fire.
A good knife folded in the pocket.
At the plot, or at Top, sowing seeds, crumbling earth,
settling plants.
The rocks. The pier. The sea worn shore-side rocks that
remain.
Her arms. Her longing to hold, and to be held tightly,
in our arms.

A Song for Joan

1   Take us to the mountain-tops where rocks are strong.
Take us to the snows where you belong.
In forests and in cloud we know that we'll be not alone;
there we'll find ourselves and you.

Take us to the mountain tops
Take us to the sea
Take us where our dreams and our imaginings fly free.

2   Take us where design and line and texture blend.
Take us where our preconceptions end.
Take us to the water's edge to stand before the wind;
there we'll find ourselves and you.

Take us to the mountain tops
Take us to the sea
Take us where our dreams and our imaginings fly free.

3   Thank you for leading us through times of gold.
Showing us the youth that's in the old.
Thank you for showing us the beauty that unfolds;
there we found ourselves and you.

I'll take you to the hills again,
New horizons see.
I'll take you where your inspiration enriches me.

Paul Heppleston
May 2005